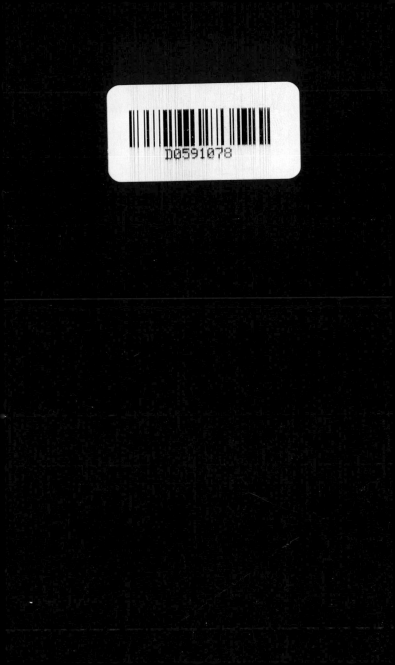

D0591078

Musical Wit

summersdale

MUSICAL WIT

With text contributed by Vicky Edwards

Illustrations by Kath Walker

Summersdale Publishers Ltd
46 West Street
Chichester
West Sussex
PO19 1RP
UK

www.summersdale.com

Printed and bound in Great Britain

ISBN: 978-1-84953-085-9

Disclaimer
Every effort has been made to attribute the quotations in this collection to the correct source. Should there be any omissions or errors in this respect we apologise and shall be pleased to make the appropriate acknowledgements in any future edition.

Substantial discounts on bulk quantities of Summersdale books are available to corporations, professional associations and other organisations. For details contact Summersdale Publishers by telephone: +44 (0) 1243 771107, fax: +44 (0) 1243 786300 or email: nicky@summersdale.com.

Musical Wit

Quips and Quotes for Music Lovers

Vicky Edwards

Illustrations by Kath Walker

For George Bennett and his glorious
George's Regis Jazz Band

Contents

Overture

'Music is the universal language of mankind' declared Henry Wadsworth Longfellow. How right he was. But actually music is even more than an all-purpose lingo. As potent as wine and as mood-altering as any narcotic, music can inspire romance, lift spirits – driving one from the depths of despair to full-on 'hairbrush karaoke' euphoria.

In this anthology of quips and quotations, you will find something that will resonate with singers, instrumentalists and music lovers alike. Encompassing wise words, rude retorts, reverent ramblings and lyrical observations, lose yourself in the utterances of some of the greatest and most infamous musical talents the world has ever known; from Coward to The King, Beethoven to Bowie, Abba to Zappa.

So crank up the volume of a favourite album, find a comfy nook in which to snuggle, and read this book while revelling in musical bliss. I hope you enjoy it – just don't expect to become musically proficient as a result. Because as that dear old warbler Pavarotti once said: 'Learning music by reading about it is like making love by mail'.

MUSICAL MUSINGS

You can't kill a
good song. It goes
on forever.

Liza Minnelli

I love Wagner, but the music I prefer
is that of a cat hung up by its tail
outside a window and trying to stick
to the panes of glass with its claws.

Charles Baudelaire

The musician is perhaps the most
modest of animals, but he is also
the proudest. It is he who invented
the sublime art of ruining poetry.

Erik Satie

Without music, life would
be a mistake.

Friedrich Nietzsche

Music is the silence
between the notes.

Claude Debussy

If music be the food of love, play on.

William Shakespeare

I wish you music to help with the burdens of life, and to help you release your happiness to others.

Ludwig van Beethoven

Music doesn't lie. If there is
something to be changed in
this world, then it can only
happen through music.

Jimi Hendrix

Music is the brandy of the damned.

George Bernard Shaw

Music is the universal
language of mankind.

Henry Wadsworth Longfellow

All deep things are song. It seems
somehow the very central essence
of us, song; as if all the rest were
but wrappages and hulls!

Thomas Carlyle

Music was my refuge. I could crawl
into the space between the notes
and curl my back to loneliness.

Maya Angelou

It was like falling in love with a woman you know is bad for you, but you love every minute with her, anyway.

Lionel Ritchie on being in the music business

FANTASTIC FANS

I've been in a public
bathroom and had
the hand come under
the stall with a paper
and pen. That sort
of thing anybody
can live without.

Helen Reddy

If my fans want to call me a
love god, then so be it!

Alexander O'Neal

***

I know that my fans want to know
who I'm sleeping with, but it's
really none of their business.

Diana Ross

***

I have been a gigantic Rolling
Stones fan since approximately
the Spanish-American War.

Dave Barry

I'm scared of going home in case
my mum meets random fans and
brings them home for a cup of tea.

Lily Allen

—◆—

I always think I'm the Tom Cruise
of music – a lot of success and
fans, but no critics, darling.

Jon Bon Jovi

I have had fans
flash me. I have
had older fans give
me their bras and
underwear onstage.

Puff Daddy

I dunno. I suppose it's because
more people write to me.

Ringo Starr on why he received more fan
mail than the rest of the Fab Four

When I first started all this, it was
mostly music fans that came along,
Stones fans. But now, I'm being
taken seriously. I've got highfalutin'
art collectors and everything!

Ronnie Wood on his new career as a portrait painter

If you like Coldplay then you're obviously very intelligent and good looking and all-around brilliant.

Chris Martin

❦

From the moment I leave my house or my hotel room, the public owns me.

Alice Cooper

SIMPLY THE BEST

I'm a born entertainer, when I open the fridge and the light comes on, I burst into song.

Robbie Williams

I've outdone anyone you can name
– Mozart, Beethoven, Bach,
Strauss. Irving Berlin, he wrote
1,001 tunes. I wrote 5,500.

James Brown

I knew that with a mouth like mine, I
just hadda be a star or something.

Barbra Streisand

We're more popular than Jesus now.

John Lennon on The Beatles

The whole business is built on ego, vanity, self-satisfaction, and it's total crap to pretend it's not.

George Michael on the music business

I'm an instant star; just add water and stir.

David Bowie

You ain't seen nothing yet, and the best is yet to come.

Michael Jackson

I am blessed with a terrific voice.
It's a God-given thing.

Roy Orbison

I don't want my body to
be a distraction from my
talent or my brain.

Shania Twain

I always thought I should
be treated like a star.

Madonna

A glamorous life is quite different to a life of luxury... For years, I was practically broke but I was still very vain and glamorous. And I still am.

Lady Gaga

If you see me once, you cannot confuse me with another.

Luciano Pavarotti

LIVE TALKIN'

After a gig I get to the hotel all psyched-up from being onstage and get stuck into *Homes and Interiors* magazine.

Gary Barlow

We're the
McDonald's of
rock. We're always
there to satisfy, and
a billion served.

Paul Stanley on KISS

When I play live it's a love fest with me and my audience. It's how I get my rocks off.

Dolly Parton

Americans want grungy people, stabbing themselves in the head on stage. They get a bright bunch like us, with deodorant on. They don't get it.

Liam Gallagher

I have fun with my clothes
onstage; it's not a concert you're
seeing, it's a fashion show.

Freddie Mercury

I've been to two stadium gigs in
my life. One was James Brown
and the other was Pink Floyd.
They both sounded the same.

Boz Burrell

I'm still trying to re-create a Ray Charles concert that I heard when I was 15 years old, and all my nerve endings were fried and transformed, and electricity shot through me.

Boz Scaggs

I would hope that we mean more to people than putting money in a church basket and saying ten Hail Marys on a Sunday. Has God played Knebworth recently?

Noel Gallagher

Have you seen U2's live
show? It's boring as hell. It's
like watching CNN.

Sharon Osbourne

Onstage I make love to 25,000
people, then I go home alone.

Janis Joplin

EVERYONE'S A CRITIC

One would hear more
vocal passion from an
ape under anaesthetic.

Morrissey on Bucks Fizz

If your lifeguard duties were as
good as your singing, a lot of
people would be drowning.

Simon Cowell to an *American Idol* contestant

The scratches in Yoko Ono
records are moments of relief.

S. A. Sachs

Give me a bad write-up
and you're dead.

Jerry Lee Lewis

The good thing about them is
that you can look at them with
the sound turned down.

George Harrison on the Spice Girls

Wagner has lovely moments but
awful quarters of an hour.

Gioacchino Rossini

Olivia Newton-John – Australia's
gift to insomniacs. It's nothing but
the blonde singing the bland.

Minnie Riperton

Let a short Act of Parliament
be passed, placing all street
musicians outside the protection
of the law, so that any citizen
may assail them with stones,
sticks, knives, pistols or bombs
without incurring any penalties.

George Bernard Shaw

We don't like their sound, and
guitar music is on the way out.

A spokesman for the Decca Recording Co.
who rejected The Beatles in 1962

Most rock journalism is people who
can't write, interviewing people who
can't talk, for people who can't read.

Frank Zappa

If my music ever got as laid-back
and mellow as his, I'd pack
it in. Or shoot myself.

Paul Weller on Eric Clapton

Interviewers could be pretty mean. In
England I was asked, 'How does it
feel to be the chubbiest Osmond?'

Jimmy Osmond

I always thought he sounded
just like Yogi Bear.

Mick Ronson on Bob Dylan

Every time I see Bono in those big
fly glasses and tight leather pants
I just can't hack it. I can't see that
as solving the world's problems.
He's crushing his testicles in
tight trousers for world peace.

John Lydon

If critics have problems with my
personal life, it's their problem.
Anybody with half a brain would
realise that it's the charts that count.

Mariah Carey

ROCK HARD

The movie *Spinal Tap* rocked my world. It's for rock what *The Sound of Music* was for hills.

Jack Black

I hate most of what constitutes
rock music, which is basically
middle-aged crap.

Sting

I am Rosa Parks with
a Gibson guitar.

Ted Nugent

Rock music should be
gross: that's the fun
of it. It gets up and
drops its trousers.

Bruce Dickinson

You know what I hate about
rock? I hate tie-dyed T-shirts.

Kurt Cobain

❧

Rock is so much fun. That's what it's
all about – filling up the chest cavities
and empty kneecaps and elbows.

Jimi Hendrix

❧

I got rabies shots for biting the
head off a bat but that's OK –
the bat had to get Ozzy shots.

Ozzy Osbourne

Everyone talks about rock
these days; the problem is
they forget about the roll.

Keith Richards

The best rock musicians are the
most exciting people in the world.

James Daly

We maintain a lead guitar and
a bass guitar, because you just
need that ker-RANG!

Ali Score

HOOKED ON CLASSICS

All the good music
has already been
written by people
with wigs and stuff.

Frank Zappa

The symphony must be like the world. It must embrace everything.

Gustav Mahler

Classical music is the kind we keep thinking will turn into a tune.

Kin Hubbard

The public doesn't want new music; the main thing it demands of a composer is that he be dead.

Arthur Honegger

Bach opens a vista
to the universe.
After experiencing
him, people feel
there is meaning
to life after all.

Helmut Walcha

I like Wagner's music better than anybody's. It is so loud that one can talk the whole time without other people hearing what one says.

Oscar Wilde

Life can't be all bad when for ten dollars you can buy all the Beethoven sonatas and listen to them for ten years.

William F. Buckley Jr

Beethoven I used to really like, and a guy called Handel wrote finger exercises that amazed me.

Suzi Quatro

Gee! This'll make Beethoven.

Walt Disney on the adaptation of Beethoven's Sixth Symphony for the film *Fantasia*

I don't know many people who put on Tchaikovsky and go ape-shit.

Pete Townshend

JAZZING IT UP

Jazz washes away the dust of everyday life.

Art Blakey

The kind of music that no matter
what you play comes out all right.

Hal Jackson on bop music

Hell, nobody knows where jazz
is going to go. There may be a
kid right now in Chitlin Switch,
Georgia, who is going to come
along and upset everybody.

Quincy Jones

Music is your own experience, your thoughts, your wisdom. If you don't live it, it won't come out of your horn.

Charlie Parker

Jazz isn't dead, it just smells funny.

Frank Zappa

One thing I like about jazz, kid, is that I don't know what's going to happen next. Do you?

Bix Beiderbecke

Playing 'bop' is like playing scrabble
with all the vowels missing.

Duke Ellington

We all do 'do, re, mi,' but you have
got to find the other notes yourself.

Louis Armstrong

Life is a lot like jazz... it's
best when you improvise.

George Gershwin

A jazz musician is
a juggler who uses
harmonies instead
of oranges.

Benny Green

GOT THE BLUES

Sounds like the
blues are composed
of feeling, finesse
and fear.

Billy Gibbons

If you don't know the blues there's
no point in picking up the guitar
and playing rock and roll or any
other form of popular music.

Keith Richards

White folks hear the blues come out,
but they don't know how it got there.

Ma Rainey

I am Aretha, upbeat, straight-
ahead, and not to be worn out by
men and left singing the blues.

Aretha Franklin

You have to understand a
bit about the poetry of the
blues to know where the
references are coming from.

Van Morrison

You can't rehearse a blues, darlin'.

Joe Williams

The blues tells a story. Every line of the blues has a meaning.

John Lee Hooker

There was a blues boom in Britain in the late 60s, but I found it very hard to go out and sing about how 'I left a steel mill in Chicago,' so I started singing about how 'I left my fish and chip shop in Brighton.'

Leo Sayer

The voice of God, if you must know, is Aretha Franklin's.

Marianne Faithfull

A guy will promise you the world and give you nothing', and that's the blues.

Otis Rush

WAXING LYRICAL

I rate Morrissey
as one of the best
lyricists in Britain.
For me, he's up there
with Bryan Ferry.

David Bowie

Cheryl, if you're reading this, I may not be as pretty as you but at least I write and SING my own songs.

Lily Allen to Cheryl Cole on her MySpace blog

A lyric has to mean something to me, something that has happened to me.

Lou Rawls

I might lie a lot but never in my lyrics.

Courtney Love

George wrote 'Taxman', and I played guitar on it. He wrote it in anger at finding out what the taxman did.

Paul McCartney

— ◆ —

The lyrics are constructed as empirically as the music. I don't set out to say anything very important.

Brian Eno

— ◆ —

For me, writing is 75 percent procrastinating and 25 percent actually sitting down and working.

Zooey Deschanel

Imagination is the key to my lyrics. The rest is painted with a little science fiction.

Jimi Hendrix

I only write about stuff that's happened to me, stuff I can't get past personally. Luckily, I'm quite self-destructive.

Amy Winehouse

Anything that is too stupid to be spoken is sung.

Voltaire

COUNTRY FOLK

All music is folk music.
I ain't never heard no
horse sing a song.

Louis Armstrong

If you talk bad about country music,
it's like saying bad things about my
momma. Them's fightin' words.

Dolly Parton

———◆———

Country music is three
chords and the truth.

Harlan Howard

———◆———

There are no bridges in folk
songs because the peasants
died building them.

Eugene Chadbourne

Country music is still your
grandpa's music, but it's also
your daughter's music.

Shania Twain

———•———

Country and western is
the music of the devil.

Rick Wakeman

———•———

A good country song takes
a page out of somebody's
life and puts it to music.

Conway Twitty

Folk is bare bones music.

Ben Harper

Country music has always been the best shrink that 15 bucks can buy.

Dierks Bentley

I only get concerned about money when the electricity goes out. Then you have to do acoustic records.

Slash

A NIGHT AT THE OPERA

People are wrong
when they say that
the opera isn't what it
used to be. It *is* what
it used to be. That's
what's wrong with it.

Noël Coward

When an opera star
sings her head off,
she usually improves
her appearance.

Victor Borge

An opera begins long before the curtain goes up and ends long after it has come down.

Maria Callas

———

Opera is where a guy gets stabbed in the back, and instead of dying, he sings.

Robert Benchley

———

I liked your opera. I think I'll set it to music.

Ludwig van Beethoven to a fellow composer

I went to watch Pavarotti once.
He doesn't like it when you join in.

Mick Miller

———•———

I have always believed that
opera is a planet where the
muses work together, join hands
and celebrate all the arts.

Franco Zeffirelli

———•———

Opera in English is, in the
main, just about as sensible
as baseball in Italian.

H. L. Mencken

I don't mind what language an opera is sung in so long as it is a language I don't understand.

Sir Edward Appleton

I love Verdi and Donizetti and all those buxom prima donnas and all the carry-ons and the rows and refusing to take curtain calls.

Noël Coward

Parsifal is the kind of opera that starts at six o'clock and after it has been running for three hours, you check your watch and it says six-twenty.

David Randolph

One can't judge Wagner's opera *Lohengrin* after a first hearing, and I certainly don't intend hearing it a second time.

Gioacchino Rossini

IT'S SHOWTIME!

Cute little babies that
fall out of swings,
These are a few of
my favourite things.

Oscar Hammerstein's working lyric
for *The Sound of Music*

I want to do a musical movie. Like *Evita*, but with good music.

Elton John

After the Rodgers and Hammerstein revolution, songs became part of the story, as opposed to just entertainments in between comedy scenes.

Stephen Sondheim

We all sing about the things
we're thinking; musicals are about
expressing those emotions that you
can't talk about. It works a real treat.

Anthony Head

They say it's not reality,
but who cares? There's too
much reality these days.

Shirley Jones in response to criticism about musicals

I'm not gay, so I don't know much
about Broadway musicals.

Norm MacDonald

I used to be this lovely juvenile
leading man who gets all the girls
and now I'm a fat evil bastard
who's only loved by his rat.
It's all gone horribly wrong!

Michael Ball

If Patti Lupone was born to play
Evita then Madonna was born to
play Patti Lupone playing Evita.

Buck Bannister

Andrew Lloyd Webber's music
is everywhere, but so is AIDS.

Malcolm Williamson

———

I've always taken *The Wizard
of Oz* very seriously, you
know. I believe in the idea of
the rainbow. And I've spent my
entire life trying to get over it.

Judy Garland

MUSIC LESSONS

Any list of advice
I have to offer to a
musician always ends
with: If it itches, go
and see a doctor.

David Bowie

You just pick a
chord, go twang, and
you've got music.

Sid Vicious

If anyone asks you what kind
of music you play, tell him 'pop'.
Don't tell him 'rock 'n' roll' or they
won't even let you in the hotel.

Buddy Holly

Master your instrument, master
the music, and then forget all
that crap and just play.

Charlie Parker

Some people think music
education is a privilege, but I think
it's essential to being human.

Jewel

External instruments are
only extensions of the
biological instrument.

Yusef Lateef

I would teach children music,
physics and philosophy; but
most importantly music, for in
the patterns of music and all the
arts are the keys of learning.

Plato

It's marvellous to be popular,
but foolish to think it will last.

Dusty Springfield

I would advise you to keep your overheads down; avoid a major drug habit; play everyday, and take it in front of other people. They need to hear it, and you need them to hear it.

James Taylor

—◆—

Learning music by reading about it is like making love by mail.

Luciano Pavarotti

—◆—

My whole trick is to keep the tune well out in front. If I play Tchaikovsky, I play his melodies and skip his spiritual struggle.

Liberace

SEX 'N' DRUGS...

A typical day in the
life of a heavy metal
musician consists of
a round of golf and
an AA meeting.

Billy Joel

As Britain's most unlikely new sex god, I sleep with lots of women... Where do you think I get my songs from?

Jarvis Cocker

I am always crazy for hot women. I am like a rabbit. I could do it anytime, anywhere.

Rod Stewart

I'd like to say work and sex have replaced drugs but there's not been enough time off work for sex.

Lily Allen

———————

Most people get into rock bands for three very simple rock and roll reasons: to get laid, to get fame and to get rich.

Bob Geldof

———————

Any guy in a band will take any girl who offers herself. Doesn't matter if she's a farmyard animal.

Chrissie Hynde

I would rather have a
cup of tea than sex.

Boy George

I wiggle my shoulders, I shake my legs, I walk up and down the stage, I hop around on one foot. But I never bump and grind. Why, that's vulgar. I'd never do anything vulgar before an audience. My mother would never allow it.

Elvis Presley

I'm just a musical prostitute, my dear.

Freddie Mercury

You can't be a sexy person
unless you have something sexy
to offer. With me, it's my voice.

Tom Jones

The problem is I'm always shouting.
That's the way I keep my voice. But
all that shouting is probably why I
can't find myself a man for keeps.

Shirley Bassey

My business is sex, drugs, rock and
roll – but as you get older and wiser
you stop a lot of the kid stuff.

Whitney Houston

Pink Floyd is one of the best bands to listen to when one is stoned on marijuana. Of course, I never inhaled.

Salman Rushdie

My justification is that most people my age spend a lot of time thinking about what they're going to do for the next five or ten years. The time they spend thinking about their life, I just spend drinking.

Amy Winehouse

... AND ROCK 'N' ROLL

Rock 'n' roll: music for
the neck downwards.

Keith Richards

Without Elvis, none of us
could have made it.

Buddy Holly

Rock 'n' roll can manage
without the sex and drugs.

Cliff Richard

I'm dealing in rock 'n' roll. I'm, like,
I'm not a bona fide human being.

Phil Spector

If you tried to give rock and roll another name, you might call it 'Chuck Berry'.

John Lennon

———•———

I can't do it. I would rather listen to hogs screwing.

Sting on the prospect of listening to old-fashioned rock 'n' roll

———•———

I once asked [John] Lennon what he thought of what I do. He said 'it's great, but it's just rock and roll with lipstick on'.

David Bowie

Rock 'n' roll: the most brutal, ugly,
desperate, vicious form of expression
it has been my misfortune to hear.

Frank Sinatra

There'll always be some
arrogant little brat who wants
to make music with a guitar.
Rock 'n' roll will never die.

Dave Edmonds

AGING ROCKERS

I'll grow old physically,
but I won't grow
old musically.

Cliff Richard

I'd rather be dead than singing 'Satisfaction' when I'm 45.

Mick Jagger

I'm rock and roll, and I'm a woman, and at a certain age you stop looking the part.

Tina Turner

Rock's so good to me. Rock is my child and my grandfather.

Chuck Berry

Because I'm 39, there's The Smiths, Radiohead, Pulp, Blur – all that quite gloomy music.

David Cameron when asked about his musical preferences

I don't feel 50. I feel not a
day over 49. It's incredible.
I'm bouncy, I feel bouncy.

David Bowie on reaching his fiftieth birthday

I must be careful not to get
trapped in the past. That's why
I tend to forget my songs.

Mick Jagger

I don't want to be one of those
middle-aged guys who turns
up with the baseball hat on
the wrong way around.

Elvis Costello

Some kids in Italy call me 'Mama Jazz'; I thought that was so cute. As long as they don't call me 'Grandma Jazz'.

Ella Fitzgerald

I was a veteran, before I was a teenager.

Michael Jackson

How can you consider flower power outdated? The essence of my lyrics is the desire for peace and harmony. That's all anyone has ever wanted. How could it become outdated?

Robert Plant

If you think you are
too old to rock 'n'
roll then you are.

Lemmy from Motörhead

GO AHEAD, PUNK...

Were it not for The Clash, punk would have been just a sneer, a safety pin and a pair of bondage trousers.

Billy Bragg

The Pistols were like my work
of art. They were my canvas.

Malcolm McLaren

━━•━━

Thank God I didn't invent anything
as banal as punk rock. It's high-
school prom crossed with pub rock.

Iggy Pop

━━•━━

Christ was a punk rocker.

Billy Idol

Punk is not dead... it's just taking a nap.

A peeved Bad Religion fan after they failed to return for an encore

━━━◆━━━

Mozart was a punk, which people seem to forget. He was a naughty, naughty boy.

Shirley Manson

━━━◆━━━

Punk is musical freedom. It's saying, doing and playing what you want.

Kurt Cobain

When the punk thing came along
and I heard my friends saying, I
hate these people with the pins
in their ears. I said, Thank God,
something got their attention.

Neil Young

The popularity of punk rock
was, in effect, due to the fact
that it made ugliness beautiful.

Malcolm McLaren

DISCO INFERNO

I think that a lifetime
of listening to disco
music is a high price
to pay for one's
sexual preference.

Quentin Crisp

The disco craze is definitely a
fad. I'm going to do something
brand new next year.

Monti Rock III

Disco is just pop music
you can dance to.

Sheena Easton

Disco deserved a better name,
a beautiful name because it
was a beautiful art form.

Barry White

Disco dancing is just
the steady thump of a
giant moron knocking
in an endless nail.

Clive James

God had to create disco
music so that I could be born
and be successful. I was
blessed. I am blessed.

Donna Summer

Disco is just jitterbug.

Fred Astaire

After we did 'Jive Talkin"
everybody said it was disco.
We didn't even know what
disco was at the time.

Barry Gibb

Disco music in the 70s was just a
call to go wild and party and dance
with no thought or conscience
or regard for tomorrow.

Martha Reeves

I'm glad to see The Clash
have gone disco. It's about time
they made some money.

David Lee Roth

RAPPERS' DELIGHT

Icelandic peoples
were the ones who
memorised the sagas...
we were the first
rappers of Europe.

Björk

My only scheme was to be a rapper.

Eminem

———◦———

And to turn it into rap wasn't
too difficult besides just rhymin'
the last words of each line.

Slick Rick

———◦———

As long as I'm around the cats in
the hip hop scene, they'll throw me
a track and I'll write a rap over it.

Ice-T

Rap is poetry to music, like beatniks
without beards and bongos.

David Lee Roth

———•———

I don't like rap music at all.
I don't think it's music. It's
just a beat and rapping.

Nina Simone

———•———

I remember being told 'Someone's
gonna make a fortune out of this
rap thing' and thinking 'no way'.

Arthur Baker

It's bad poetry executed by people that can't sing. That's my definition of rap.

Pete Steele

Rap is poetry set to music. But to me it's like a jackhammer.

Bette Midler

I rap in such a way where the
hood can respect it but I can sit
in front of a white executive and
spit the exact same verse and he'll
understand at least 80 per cent of it.

Kanye West

When you do rap albums, you
got to train yourself. You got
to constantly be in character.

Tupac Shakur

MUSICALLY MODEST

I love to sing, and I
love to drink scotch.
Most people
would rather hear
me drink scotch.

George Burns

I don't know anything about music.
In my line you don't have to.

Elvis Presley

———

I think I sound like Barry White.

Gloria Gaynor

———

It's a noise we make, that's all. You
can be nice and call it music.

Mick Jagger

I don't even know if I can take credit
for writing 'Cliffs of Dover'... it
was just there for me one day...
literally wrote [it] in five minutes.

Eric Johnson

———•———

I am a servant of the music...
and if I get caught up in ego,
I'll lose everything... it'll burn
and that's a guarantee.

Eric Clapton

Anybody with a sense of humour is going to put on my album and laugh from beginning to end.

Eminem

We're the world's ugliest
band. When we play I expect
to find puke in the aisles.

Bobby Colomby on his band Blood, Sweat and Tears

———•———

You know, a song is like a kid.
You bring it up. And sometimes
something you thought was going
to be fantastic, by the time it's
finished, is a bit of a disappointment.

Phil Collins

Yeah. I'm amateurish. I can play enough to write a song, or strum on a little guitar to write out a song. But, I don't play well at all. I wouldn't even attempt for a second to play in public.

Ben E. King

At the end of the Beatles, I really was done in for the first time in my life. Until then, I really was a kind of cocky sod.

Paul McCartney

When I am sad I sing, then
others can be sad with me.

Fred Allen

I don't deserve a Songwriters
Hall of Fame Award. But
fifteen years ago, I had a brain
operation and I didn't deserve
that, either. So I'll keep it.

Quincy Jones

Give me a laundry list and
I'll set it to music.

Giaocchino Rossini

TUNEFULLY TALENTED

There's a basic rule
which runs through all
kinds of music, kind
of an unwritten rule.
I don't know what it
is. But I've got it.

Ronnie Wood

A good song should make you wanna tap your foot and get with your girl. A great song should destroy cop cars and set fire to the suburbs.

Tom Morello

For a long time I wasn't listening to music... I would get that feeling that I'm not alive 'cause I'm not making it. And if it was good, I hated it 'cause I wasn't doing it. And if it was bad, I was furious 'cause I could've done it better.

John Lennon

I hate straight singing. I have to change a tune to my own way of doing it. That's all I know.

Billie Holiday

I just fell out of bed one morning and had the tune for 'Yesterday'. I don't know how I got that. I just got it. And I thought, I like that one.

Paul McCartney

I have a machine in my throat
that gets into many people's
ears and affects them.

Judy Garland

———

People often remark that I'm pretty
lucky. Luck is only important in
so far as getting the chance to
sell yourself at the right moment.
After that, you've got to have
talent and know how to use it.

Frank Sinatra

What have I got? No looks, no money, no education. Just talent.

Sammy Davis Jr

I have a definite talent for convincing people to try something new. I am a good salesman. When I'm on form, I can sell anything.

Brian Eno

I sing like I feel.

Ella Fitzgerald

It was such a turning point to
find that I had a talent and I had
something to contribute, somewhere.

Gwen Stefani

❦

I was always musical – yelling
when I was a baby, singing into a
brush and singing in the shower.

Susan Boyle

INSTRUMENTS
OF TORTURE

Like two skeletons
copulating on a
corrugated tin roof.

Thomas Beecham on the sound a harpsichord makes

The piano is
a monster that
screams when you
touch its teeth.

Andrés Segovia

The Irish gave the bagpipes
to the Scots as a joke, but the
Scots haven't seen the joke yet.

Oliver Herford

Madam, you have between your
legs an instrument capable of
giving pleasure to thousands,
and all you can do is scratch it!

Thomas Beecham to a lady cellist

I understand the inventor of the
bagpipes was inspired when he
saw a man carrying an indignant,
asthmatic pig under his arm.
Unfortunately, the man-made
sound never equalled the purity of
the sound achieved by the pig.

Alfred Hitchcock

Q: What is the definition
of a real gentleman?
A: Somebody who knows how to
play the trombone but doesn't.

Anonymous

If thine enemy wrongs thee, buy
each of his children a drum.

Chinese proverb

Violin playing has to sound divine.
Your playing sounds human.

Anonymous

Get up from that piano.
You hurtin' its feelings

Jelly Roll Morton

When she started to play,
Steinway came down personally
and rubbed his name off the piano.

Bob Hope on Phyllis Diller

When an instrument fails on stage it
mocks you and must be destroyed.

Trent Reznor

BOLD AS BRASS

Brass bands are
all very well in their
place – outdoors and
several miles away.

Thomas Beecham

I used to look at these pictures of trumpeters pointing their instrument to the ceiling. Stunning pictures, but if you play the trumpet and point it upwards, all the spit comes back into your mouth!

Humphrey Lyttelton

The tuba is certainly the most intestinal of instruments – the very lower bowel of music.

Peter De Vries

The nerves are a problem on trumpet, because when you mess up everyone can hear it. Just remember most people are too polite to say anything about it.

Wynton Marsalis

In 'thinking up' music I usually have some kind of a brass band with wings on it in back of my mind.

Charles Ives

You can't play anything on a horn that Louis hasn't played.

Miles Davis on Louis Armstrong

One bites into the brass mouthpiece
of his wooden cudgel, and the
other blows his cheeks out on a
French horn. Do you call that art?

Franz Schubert

I stole everything I ever heard, but
mostly I stole from the horns.

Ella Fitzgerald

A frisky spirit makes
my trombone sing.

Chris Barber

BEAT IT!

I'm not a singer
who plays a bit of
drums. I'm a drummer
that sings a bit.

Phil Collins

Dealing with a drummer isn't
that much different from dealing
with someone from IT.

Tony Ridder

Seemed to me that drumming was
the best way to get close to God.

Lionel Hampton

I told people I was a drummer
before I even had a set, I
was a mental drummer.

Keith Moon

A master drummer
must have seven eyes.

African proverb

Percussion is like walking through the forest. You can't possibly see it all, there are endless possibilities of what you can do.

John Bergamo

Give him a long drum solo and he'll just blow the place up.

Joe Morello on Buddy Rich

You know the drum was the first instrument besides the human voice.

Billy Higgins

A good drummer listens
as much as he plays.

Indian proverb

To get your playing more
forceful, hit the drums harder.

Keith Moon

I have never taken more than two
weeks to record an album (on
drums) throughout my career.

Ginger Baker

What's the last thing a drummer says in a band? 'Hey guys, why don't we try one of my songs?'

Dave Grohl

TINKLING THE IVORIES

The piano is the
easiest instrument to
play in the beginning,
and the hardest to
master in the end.

Vladimir Horowitz

The pianoforte is the most important of all musical instruments: its invention was to music what the invention of printing was to poetry.

George Bernard Shaw

There is nothing to it. You only have to hit the right notes at the right time and the instrument plays itself.

Johann Sebastian Bach on playing the organ

Without a piano I don't know
how to stand, don't know
what to do with my hands.

Norah Jones

The piano is able to
communicate the subtlest
universal truths by means of
wood, metal and vibrating air.

Kenneth Miller

When I first fell in love with the piano,
I knew it was me. I was dying to play.

Alicia Keys

I'm an interpreter of stories. When I perform it's like sitting down at my piano and telling fairy stories.

Nat King Cole

If I'm going to hell, I'm going there playing the piano.

Jerry Lee Lewis

Pianos are such noble instruments – they're either upright or grand.

Anonymous

I guess, you know, if I didn't
make it with the piano, I guess I
would've been the biggest bum.

Thelonious Monk

I sit down to the piano regularly
at nine o'clock in the morning and
Mesdames les Muses have learned
to be on time for that rendezvous.

Pyotr Ilyich Tchaikovsky

STRINGING ALONG

My violin is called
Kylie as she
sounds great and is
perfectly formed.

Nigel Kennedy

When you strum a guitar you
have everything – rhythm,
bass, lead and melody.

David Gilmour

Technically, I'm not a guitar player;
all I play is truth and emotion.

Jimi Hendrix

A table, a chair, a
bowl of fruit and
a violin; what else
does a man need
to be happy?

Albert Einstein

What I do now is all my dad's fault,
because he bought me a guitar as
a boy, for no apparent reason.

Rod Stewart

Guitar playing is a release,
liberation, put simply it is freedom.

William Christopher Handy

Have you been playing a long time?

Queen Elizabeth II to Eric Clapton

Violin playing is a physical art with great traditions behind it.

Vanessa Mae

Love is like a violin. The music may stop now and then, but the strings remain forever.

June Masters Bacher

I was the same kind of father as I
was a harpist – I played by ear.

Harpo Marx

The cello is like a beautiful woman
who has not grown older, but
younger with time, more slender,
more supple, more graceful.

Pablo Casals

Wes Montgomery played
impossible things on the guitar
because it was never pointed out
to him that they were impossible.

Ronnie Scott

If I don't practice one day, I know
it; two days, the critics know it;
three days, the public knows it.

Jascha Heifetz

HAVING A POP

A lot of pop music is about stealing pocket money from children.

Ian Anderson

Pop music should be treated
with the disrespect it deserves.

Bob Geldof

I think pop music has done more for
oral intercourse than anything else
that ever happened, and vice versa.

Frank Zappa

Extraordinary how
potent cheap music is.

Noël Coward

Our first single, 'Ticket To Ride', was a kind of half hit, half flop: in some places it was number one, in others it was ashtray material.

Karen Carpenter

When I performed I was thinking, you all look like you should be seeing Phil Collins. Then I thought, hang on, I sound like Phil Collins.

David Bowie on his 80s pop sound

I know about Kylie [Minogue] and Robbie [Williams] and *Pop Idol* and stuff like that. You can't get away from that when you hit the shore, so I know all about the cruise ship entertainment aspect of British pop.

David Bowie

Modern music is as
dangerous as narcotics.

Pietro Mascagni

We're in the dark ages if J-Lo can
have a music career because of her
ass. And let's face it, that's it.

Jack Black

I remember hearing 'SOS' on the radio in the States and realising that it was ABBA. But it was too late, because I was already transported by it.

Pete Townshend

I've never believed that pop
music is escapist trash. There's
always a darkness in it, even
amidst great pop music.

Thom Yorke

***

He has a woman's name and
wears make-up. How original.

Alice Cooper on Marilyn Manson

Do I listen to pop music because
I'm miserable or am I miserable
because I listen to pop music?

Nick Hornby

Pop is actually my least
favourite kind of music,
because it lacks real depth.

Christina Aguilera

BRINGING DOWN
THE BATON

If anyone has
conducted a Beethoven
performance and then
doesn't have to go to an
osteopath, then there's
something wrong.

Simon Rattle

If I look a buffoon while I'm
transported by a piece of music,
then so be it; I don't care.

**Sue Perkins on training as a conductor
on the BBC's *Maestro* programme**

I don't feel that the conductor
has real power. The orchestra
has the power, and every member
of it knows instantaneously
if you're just beating time.

Itzhak Perlman

The conductor's stand is
not a continent of power, but
rather an island of solitude.

Riccardo Muti

I find little in the works of
Beethoven, Berlioz, Wagner
and others when they are
led by a conductor who
functions like a windmill.

Franz Liszt

Show me an orchestra that
likes its conductor and I'll show
you a lousy conductor.

Goddard Lieberson

All the conductor has to do is
stand back and try not to get in the
way. Mozart is doing all the work.

Colin R. Davis

There are two golden rules for an orchestra: start together and finish together. The public doesn't give a damn what goes on in between.

Thomas Beecham

Anyone who thinks conducting is just waving their arms around is going to get a rude awakening if they try it out.

Bradley Walsh on training as a conductor on the BBC's *Maestro* programme

Being a conductor
is kind of a hybrid
profession because
most fundamentally, it
is being someone who
is a coach, a trainer,
an editor, a director.

Michael Tilson Thomas

THE FOOD OF LOVE
AND HEARTBREAK

I want to write songs
that are so sad, the
kind of sad where
you take someone's
little finger and break
it in three places.

Nick Cave

I detest 'love lyrics'. I think one of
the causes of bad mental health in
the United States is that people
have been raised on 'love lyrics'.

Frank Zappa

It is either singing or a bit of
romance, and I don't get the
romance so I will continue singing.

Shirley Bassey

Music is the medicine
of the breaking heart.

Leigh Hunt

Where words fail, music speaks.

Hans Christian Andersen

Music makes one feel so romantic –
at least it always gets on one's nerves
– which is the same thing nowadays.

Oscar Wilde

Music is what feelings sound like.

Anonymous

Music is love in search of a word.

Sidney Lanier

My heart, which is so full to
overflowing, has often been
solaced and refreshed by
music when sick and weary.

Martin Luther

Music is the great arbiter of the world, the key to central harmony, and a necessary requirement of human emotion.

Hsun Tzu

Music is the key to the female heart.

Johann G. Seume

Music is the shorthand of emotion.

Leo Tolstoy

A love song is just a
caress set to music.

Sigmund Romberg

ARTISTIC TEMPERAMENT

It is like trying to compare Coca Cola to champagne.

Maria Callas on comparisons made between her and Renata Tebaldi

I've had singing lessons
and plan to show off.

Geri Halliwell

⊷⊶

I get nervous when I don't get
nervous. If I'm nervous I know I'm
going to have a good show.

Beyoncé Knowles

⊷⊶

You can't arrest me, I'm a rock star.

John Lydon

I don't know how many times someone has come up to me and said, 'Hey, let's dance!' I hate dancing. God, it's stupid.

David Bowie

All my concerts had no sounds in them; they were completely silent. People had to make up their own music in their minds!

Yoko Ono

Because it was full of boring people.

Björk on why she smashed all the
windows in a Reykjavik disco

———•———

Some say I have a beautiful
voice, some say I have not. It
is a matter of opinion. All I
can say, those who don't like it
shouldn't come to hear me.

Maria Callas

———•———

I just don't like the idea of her
singing my songs. Who the hell
does she thinks she is? The world
doesn't need another Streisand!

Barbra Streisand on Diana Ross

I won't be happy till I'm
as famous as God.

Madonna